Praise for BIRDS O

A haunting gallery of indigenous ~~p~~ .... ~~Peru~~, most anonymous, is finally mapped out by Quechua poet Odi Gonzales in this admirable collection. I was reminded of W.G. Sebald's exploration of the Nazi ghosts sprinkled all over the German landscape. Through Lynn Levin's lucid renditions, the painters' eyes become ours, and so does Cusco, the heart of the Inca Empire, which, under the Spaniards, became one of Dante's circles of hell. Among these artists, dignity and resistance were synonymous. And, from misery, they drew the contours of a new civilization. Poetry, Gonzales persuades us, is a tool to unveil the past, to come face to face with history.

—Ilan Stavans, editor of
The FSG Book of Twentieth-Century Latin American Poetry

Powerful, stunningly beautiful, teeming with indigenous life like the paintings of the seventeenth-century Quechua artists who appropriated and transformed the art and religion of their colonizers, Odi Gonzales' poetry celebrates the culture of his native Peru. This bilingual edition offers readers an eye-opening, rich and transformative experience. Lynn Levin's translation captures the power and nuanced registers of Odi Gonzales' *tour de force:* a gift to Anglophone readers!

—Thalia Pandiri
Professor of Classics and Comparative Literature, Smith College
Editor-in-Chief, *Metamorphoses*

With the publication of *Birds on the Kiswar Tree,* translator Lynn Levin has faithfully introduced an important world poet into the English language. In the nativist spirit of César Vallejo and the Cusqueño School of resistance painting, Odi Gonzales' poems articulate and negotiate the harrowing terrain of Peruvian cultural identity. Woven of Spanish Catholic and indigenous Quechua colors, these pages shimmer like angels in an Andean Eden! As necessary acts of recovery, revelation, and love, Gonzales' poems build a multidimensional temple in honor of the cunning and resilience of a people who whispered their very souls into their art.

—Chad Sweeney, author of *Parable of Hide and Seek*

Birds on the Kiswar Tree is a powerful, poignant and compelling series of poems, truly a verbal museum or gallery of works by underappreciated artists quietly defying their oppressors. "I am the apocryphal archangel...the bastard bereft of my heritage," exclaims one illiterate Quechua painter who speaks in these pages—one of the indigenous artists of the Cusqueñan School of the late 16th and early 17th centuries in the subjugated Inca kingdom of the Andean highlands. "I am the Anonymous One of The Almudena Church," declares another of these *"artisans / [who] did not know / how to sign their own names or read or write"* and yet filled the colonial churches of their conquerors with glorious visions, taking the Christian myths imposed by Spanish force upon the Quechua people and transposing their signs and scenes into indigenous natural historical and devotional terms. Peruvian-Quechua poet Odi Gonzales has dramatized the voices of these quiet but persistently subversive painter-personae, their colonial overlords, and the depicted biblical figures themselves; and translator Lynn Levin has faithfully rendered these voices into English. That a Peruvian poet can resurrect such voices now bespeaks the ultimate survival of Quechua culture which, though it may seem exotic to some readers, speaks through these poems to anyone who has lived—historically or imaginatively—under a repressive regime and who seeks a means of artistic resistance.

—Carolyne Wright, American Book Award,
Blue Lynx Prize, National Translation Award

Odi Gonzales's tableaux and *retablos* are as rooted as the *kiswar* tree and as eccentric as its birds in flight. Indigenous (originating there) but also syncretic (animated by difference), these poems take us beyond the exotic Cusco of the tourist-poet and towards the double (or multiple)-voiced space of the auto-ethnographic writer/archivist/witness. The Cusco School here refers not just to Andean artists' subversive remixing of Roman Catholic iconography during the colonial era, but also to a poetics that (like Vallejo's) values the local, the vernacular, the untranslatable, and the complexly sited, both as an aesthetic opportunity and as a political necessity. Gonzales's incursion into art history becomes a means of mapping and interrogating social space, of unfolding the lyric poem in all its postcolonial weight and communal energy (*synkretizein* = to combine against a common enemy). Like the legendary 17th-century Quechua chronicler and artist Guamán Poma, whose drafts are among those recovered and glossed in these pages,

Gonzales understands the writer as a double agent, working both inside and outside official culture. Writing here is an act of witness *and* revision, inasmuch as words (in Spanish, in Quechua, in thought) can complicate existing ideologies and beliefs, teasing out a paradoxically unadorned baroque: *"this canvas/is profane* [...] there are no embellishments." In Lynn Levin's precise yet sinuous translations, which read like an organic extension of the book's unorthodox documentary poetics, Gonzales is revealed to us as a poet of subtle music and radical imaginings, tracing an alternative hemispheric history in, but also against, the American grain.

—Urayoán Noel, poet and scholar, SUNY Albany

BIRDS ON THE KISWAR TREE

BIRDS ON THE KISWAR TREE

Poems by Odi Gonzales

A Bilingual Spanish/English Edition
Translated by Lynn Levin

2LP TRANSLATIONS

NEW YORK

www.2leafpress.org

P.O. Box 4378
Grand Central Station
New York, New York 10163-4378
editor@2leafpress.org
www.2leafpress.org

2LEAF PRESS
is an imprint of the
Intercultural Alliance of Artists & Scholars, Inc. (IAAS),
a NY-based nonprofit 501(c)(3) organization that promotes
multicultural literature and literacy.
www.theiaas.org

Book design and layout: Gabrielle David

Library of Congress Control Number: 2013958333
ISBN-13: 978-1-940939-24-7 (Paperback)
ISBN-13: 978-1-940939-25-4 (eBook)

10 9 8 7 6 5 4 3 2 1

Published in the United States of America

First Edition | First Printing

La Escuela de Cusco by Odi Gonzales was first published by Ediciones el Santo Oficio-Gráficos, Santiago de Surco, Peru. Copyright © 2005 Ediciones el Santo Oficio Gráficos S. R. L.

2LEAF PRESS trade distribution is handled by University of Chicago Press / Chicago Distribution Center (www.press.uchicago.edu) 773.702.7010. Titles are also available for corporate, premium, and special sales. Please direct inquiries to the UCP Sales Department, 773.702.7248.

A María Nieves Arcángel, Lauren y Benjamin
(To María Nieves Arcángel, Lauren and Benjamin)

Table of Contents

Pintureros
Artisans

MUSEO DE INDIAS
The Museum of the Indies

LA SIXTINA DE AMERICA
The Sistine Chapel of America

Acknowledgments

WE GRATEFULLY ACKNOWLEDGE the publications in which these translations, sometimes in earlier versions, first appeared:

The Dirty Goat
"The Procession of the Corpus Christi" / "La procesión del corpus," "The Paradise of the Vaulted Ceiling" / "El paraíso de la bóveda baída," "Suzanna and the Elders" / "Susana y los viejos," and "The Watcher of the Skies" / "El observador de los cielos"

E-Verse Radio
"Baradiel Loading Gunpowder into His Harquebus" and "The Last Supper"

Mandorla
"Mary Anoints the Feet of Jesus," "Writers Recount the Life and Deeds of Saint Catherine of Siena," "Judgment, Salvation and the Suffering of the Damned," and "The Army of God"

Metamorphoses
"Apprentice Painters"/"Los aprendices," "God Shows Paradise to Adam and Eve"/"Dios muestra paraíso a Adán y Eva," and "The Prodigal Son"/"El hijo pródigo"

Michigan Quarterly Review
"Matrimonio de Don Martín de Loyola con Doña Beatriz Ñusta"/"The Marriage of Don Martín de Loyola and Doña Beatriz Ñusta," "El taller de Nazareth"/"The Workshop of Nazareth," and "San José, la Virgen y el Niño"/"Saint Joseph, the Virgin and the Child"

Off the Coast
"Adoration of the Shepherds"/"Adoración de los pastores"

Parthenon West Review
"Saint Isidore, the Farmer"/"San Isidro labrador" and "Descent of the Virgin to the Sunturwasi"/"Descendimiento de la Virgen en sunturwasi"

PennSound/PennSonido
"The Last Supper"/"La ultima cena," "Baradiel Loading Gunpowder into His Harquebus"/"Baradiel cargando con pólvora su arcabús," "Descent of the Virgin to the Sunturwasi"/"Descendimiento de la Virgen en sunturwasi," and "The Marriage of Don Martín de Loyola and Doña Beatriz Ñusta"/"Matrimonio de Don Martín de Loyola con Doña Beatriz Ñusta"

Per Contra
"The Last Supper"/"La última cena"

Poetry Miscellany
"Baradiel Loading Gunpowder into His Harquebus"/"Baradiel cargando con pólvora su arcabús," "The Fallen Woman"/"La adúltera," "The Unknown Artist/His Early Works"/"El pintor/Los artificios," "Portrait of Don Manuel Mollinedo y Angulo, Bishop of Cusco"/"Retrato de Don Manuel Mollinedo y Angulo obispo del Cusco," and "The Expulsion from Paradise"/"La Expulsión del paraíso"

The Portable Boog Reader 4
"Studies of Angels" / "Estudios de ángeles" and "Lamentation of Mary before the Body of Christ" / "Lamentación de María ante el cadáver de Cristo"

The Willow's Whisper
O'Mahony, Jill and Micheal O'hAodha, ed. UK: Cambridge Scholars Publishing, 2011. "The Last Supper"/"La última cena" and "The Marriage of Don Martín de Loyola and Doña Beatriz Ñusta" / "Matrimonio de Don Martín de Loyola con Doña Beatriz Ñusta"

Translator's Notes

I FIRST MET ODI GONZALES via a phone call in 2002. I had been planning a trip to Peru, mostly aimed at seeing Cusco, Machu Picchu, and pursuing language study, but I also wished to meet some Peruvian writers and possibly translate them. A fortunate chain of emails led me to Gonzales who happened to be in the US at the time, pursuing graduate studies at the University of Maryland. After three breathtaking weeks in the Andes (the sights were amazing and so was the altitude), I returned, began corresponding with Gonzales and translating some poems from his earlier books, *Almas en Pena* (1998) and *Valle Sagrado* (1993).

Gonzales had mentioned to me that he was devoting much of his time to a book of poems that centered on Cusco's artistic heritage, and soon after it was published he mailed me a copy of *La Escuela de Cusco* (Lima, Perú: Ediciones el Santo Oficio-Gráficos S. R. L., 2005). I immediately found myself in a gallery of exciting and subversive poems. In visiting museums and churches in Cusco, I had learned from the guides that colonial-era Quechua artists often painted native flora and fauna in their religious paintings as a way of rebelling against Spanish domination. I remember seeing one such painting in Korikancha or the Temple of the Sun (converted into a church by the Spanish) in which an indigenous artist had painted native cantu flowers into the brocade of a bishop's robes and also carved the cantu flower into the Corinthian-style columns that decorated the picture frame. I was very taken by this act of resistance, and when I saw that Odi Gonzales's collection was, in large part, dedicated to describing this sort of artistic rebellion, I began to translate a few of the poems. I started the project in 2006, not really intending to translate the whole book, but it got so that I couldn't wait to discover the next poem, and eventually I translated the whole book.

What emerges in Odi Gonzales's *Birds on the Kiswar Tree* is poetry collection as living and talking museum. The poet takes us on a tour of lyric poems based on the works of religious fine art painted in the Mannerist style by indigenous and mestizo painters during Peru's colonial period. Through interlaced voices—those of the painters, the biblical figures in the paintings, Spanish church officials, a critical modern-day museum guide, and the poet himself—the poems enact the piety and secret rebelliousness of these artists. Painting flourished during the sixteenth and seventeenth centuries in Peru when Spain sent highly accomplished painters, some of them painter-priests, to the Andes in order to evangelize the people through art and art instruction. The Church, however, put severe restrictions on the native artists: they were permitted to paint only religious subjects. The artists responded by producing work that was pious, syncretistic, and subversive. In hidden nooks in churches, Quechua artists painted angels with harquebuses; they furnished the Garden of Eden with Andean birds, trees, and flowers; and, perhaps most famously, one painter set the table of the Last Supper with native foods, including a roasted guinea pig *(cuy),* a staple of the Andean diet. Because most of the colonial-era Quechua artists resided in and around the former Inca capital of Cusco, they came to be known as the School of Cusco painters, hence the original title of Gonzales's collection. Ironically, although the artists were highly skilled, they were often illiterate and anonymous. Gonzales's poems give these artists a voice. In keeping with the poetry-book-as-museum concept, Gonzales presents the titles of the poems as museum wall labels. The poems generally bear the titles of the actual paintings and are accompanied by the artist's name (or with the attribution "anonymous" when the artist was unknown) and the location of the work.

The title of the translated edition of the poems, *Birds on the Kiswar*

Tree, reflects the proliferation of bird imagery in the paintings and the poems. The kiswar tree, which is also known as the *quenua* or *quisuar* depending on the region, has curving branches well-suited for nesting. Birds commonly perch atop the tree.

Translating these poems offered several unique challenges. The poet employs many highly specific terms relating to church architecture and art practice, and I found myself wandering through the websites of Spanish and Peruvian museums and churches in order to capture the correct terms. In the course of translating, I had to acquaint myself with the lives of saints and several obscure non-canonical angels. And while I found it a boon to discover images of the actual paintings in books or online, I also learned the drawbacks of being too literal. Gonzales explained to me that in addition to the travel and research he undertook to write the poems, he also had to conjure up some of the works from memory, add imagery to some, and imagine others for which no originals, copies, or images exist: this is because a significant number of works by School of Cusco painters have been stolen or destroyed over the centuries. In envisioning and describing the religious and regional scenes, Gonzales, in a sense, becomes via language a School of Cusco painter. With all respect for the primacy of the poet's imagination, I still yearned to see the actual works. I encountered some lucky finds online, and I was able to consult a remarkable text, *Historia del arte cusqueño: pintores cusqueños de la colonia* by Teófilo Benavente Velarde (Municipalidad Provincial del Cusco, 1995). Gonzales also used this text as a resource. This art book enabled me to see many of the paintings and provided key biographical information for many of the artists.

I spent a good deal of time online and pouring through travel books in order to research place names—Gonzales refers to many small villages in Peru's Sacred Valley—and locations that connect back to battles the Incas waged against the Spanish. Discovering the historical significance of the *sunturwasi* (an Inca armory) and Vilcabamba (the site of a Quechua uprising against the Spanish), for example, deepened the meaning of the poems. Through all my researches, Odi Gonzales was there to help me with locations, tricky vocabulary issues, references to Andean agricultural practices, legends, and Quechua religious and cultural beliefs. For example, I learned that the Quechuas believe that a person who has two whorls in his hair is destined to be stubborn. The poet noted that he has two such whorls! And who better to explain all these terms and concepts to me than Gonzales, who is not only a poet but a native speaker of Quechua and a specialist in Quechua culture. I hope that readers will find the glossaries I have included with each poem to be of help.

This was a collaborative translation. Odi Gonzales, who is trilingual in Quechua, Spanish, and English, reviewed my drafts and revisions for accuracy. I approached the translation of these poems as a poet, but I did not take liberties. The speakers in these poems are earnest and yearn to be heard and understood. Loose or subjective interpretations of these poems would not do. Therefore, I strived to echo the original texts as closely as possible. In addition to fine-tuning my translations, our collaborative process had an interesting side effect: as he reviewed my translations, Odi Gonzales found the opportunity to re-enter and slightly modify some of his original texts. For this reason, the Spanish versions here are, in small ways, different from those in the original publication.

I did my best to stay true to Gonzales's sense, spirit, and style. If Gonzales included alliterations, I tried to alliterate. If Gonzales used short lines or compressed language, I tried to reproduce that. When a speech by a powerful church figure felt stern and threatening in Spanish, I tried to make it sound that way in English. If the words of an angel sounded mysterious and commanding, then I tried to convey that in my lines. Much of the power and charm of the poems in *Birds on the Kiswar Tree* resides in their foreignness, their exoticism. I wanted to bring that through in the translations. In some cases that meant retaining the native names of things and then defining those terms in the glossary. While the poems are steeped in Quechua culture and are exotic in many ways, they also speak to anyone who lives or, historically or imaginatively, has lived under a repressive regime and who seeks a means of artistic resistance.

Collaborating with Odi Gonzales on these translations proved to be one of the most rewarding intellectual experiences I have ever had. At first we worked via email when Gonzales was in Peru. The poet would reply with corrections and explanations. When Gonzales moved back to New York to teach Quechua language and culture and prehispanic literature of the Andean region at New York University, our collaboration became more focused and more fun. We embarked upon a series of face-to-face meetings in New York. I was delighted when Gonzales praised my renderings of poems. I was grateful when he guided me toward clarifications, pushed me to find a better word, or explained aspects of Quechua culture. In the final poem in this collection, Gonzales writes that "the meeting of two men/is the meeting of two rivers." So, too, is the collaboration of translator and poet for the process represents a confluence of spirit and understanding.⌘

—Lynn Levin
Southampton, Pennsylvania

Noticia

LA ESCUELA CUSQUEÑA DE PINTURA se gestó a finales del siglo XVI e inicios del XVII con la llegada de los maestros europeos Bernardo Demócrito Bitti, Angelino Medoro y Mateo Pérez de Alesio que permanecieron en la región andina (1575-1610) estableciéndose en las principales ciudades del virreynato: Lima, Cusco, Arequipa, Huamanga, Potosí, Chuquisaca, La Paz y Quito.

A solicitud de las órdenes religiosas que se asentaron tras la Conquista, los tres pintores italianos—con larga actividad artística en España—llegan para "colaborar en la tarea de evangelización de los indios mediante el sistema visual de los cuadros", introduciendo en estas tierras el llamado Manierismo, movimiento artístico que ya llegaba a su fin en Europa.

Seguidores de la escuela de Miguel Angel, Rafael, El Greco, Caravaggio, Murillo, entre otros, los maestros europeos—junto al florentino Pedro Santángel y los españoles Juan de Mosquera y fray Diego de Ocaña—implementaron en Cusco talleres de arte frecuentados por discípulos mayoritariamente indígenas y mestizos. En este contexto de transición, la labor del cronista y dibujante quechua Felipe Guamán Poma de Ayala fue determinante. Otra figura central del naciente movimiento pictórico fue, sin duda, el docto obispo de Cusco Manuel Mollinedo y Angulo, clérigo madrileño que arribó a las Indias en misión pastoral y terminó promoviendo un florecimiento cultural en la capital de los Incas. Fue él quien trajo consigo una gran cantidad de copias de pinturas y grabados europeos.

Artistas que no pudieron firmar sus cuadros—por desconocer la escritura—los llamados pintores indios fueron en mayoría anónimos, situación que no fue un veto para generar una escuela, acaso la contribución pictórica sudamericana más importante a la pintura universal. ⌘

—Odi Gonzales
Cusco, Perú

Author's Note

THE CUSQUEÑAN SCHOOL OF PAINTING was born in the late sixteenth and early seventeenth centuries with the arrival of the European masters Bernardo Democrito Bitti, Angelino Medoro, and Mateo Pérez de Alesio who settled in the Andean region between 1575 and 1610, taking up residence in the principal cities of the viceroyalty: Lima, Cusco, Arequipa, Huamanga, Potosí, Chuquisaca, La Paz and Quito.

Under the auspices of the religious orders that were established in the New World after the Conquest, the three Italian painters—who had been very active in Spain—"collaborated in the work of evangelizing the Indians through the visual system of paintings" and introduced in those regions the so-called Mannerist movement, an artistic style that was coming to an end in Europe.

Disciples of the schools of Michelangelo, Raphael, El Greco, Caravaggio, Murillo, and others, the three European masters—in association with the Florentine painter Pedro Santángel and the Spaniards Juan de Mosquera and Brother Diego de Ocaña—established workshops in Cusco, which were frequented by their followers, who were mostly indigenous and mestizo. In this time of transition, the work of the Quechua chronicler and illustrator Felipe Guamán Poma played a key role. Another central figure of the nascent art movement was, undoubtedly, the noted Bishop of Cusco Manuel Mollinedo y Angulo, a cleric from Madrid who arrived in the Indies on a pastoral mission and ended up promoting a cultural blossoming in the capital of the Incas. It was he who brought with him a huge quantity of copies of European paintings and engravings.

Artists who could not sign their canvases—on account of illiteracy—the so-called Indian painters were, for the most part, anonymous. Yet that situation did not stop them from giving birth to an artistic school which was, perhaps, the most important South American contribution to world painting.⌘

—Odi Gonzales
Cusco, Peru

PINTUREROS
Artisans

Este paraíso está habitado por ángeles
es un paraíso de pájaros parlantes

This paradise is inhabited by angels
it is a paradise of chattering birds

—Teresa Gisbert

LA ÚLTIMA CENA

Catedral de Cusco

Atribuido a ciegas
al Círculo Tenebrista de San Blas
al Anónimo de Maras
al Maestro de Taray
                         poco
tengo que decir:
                    el lienzo
salió de mi mano: yo
pinté, doré y estofé la Santa Cena

               Aquí
el taimado pintor indio — el Anónimo de la Catedral —
en un rapto delirante
añadió por cuenta propia
potajes y viandas de su cosecha:

            en lugar
del consagrado pan — sin levadura —
dispuse en la mesa pascual
cuy asado, rocotos rellenos,
               ají
como si el cenáculo no fuera en Tierra Santa
               si no
en una fonda cusqueña, digamos
            "La Chola"

THE LAST SUPPER
Cathedral of Cusco

Blindly attributed
to the Tenebrist Circle of San Blas
to the Anonymous One of Maras
to the Master of Taray
              one thing
I have to say:
          this painting
came from my own hands: I alone
painted, gilded, glazed the Sacred Meal

          Here
the cunning Indian painter—the Anonymous One of the Cathedral—
in a flight of ecstasy
added on his own initiative
his favorite foods:

      in place of
the holy bread—flat and unleavened—
I set upon on the paschal table
roasted cuy, stuffed peppers
         spicy pepper
as if the Upper Room were not in the Holy Land
        but more likely
in a cozy tavern in Cusco, let's say
        "La Chola"

NOTES

Maras is a small Andean town in the Sacred Valley of Peru in the Cusco region. Before the Spanish conquest, this region was the center of the Inca civilization.

Taray is a village in the Sacred Valley of Peru.

Cuy is guinea pig, a staple of the Andean diet.

Chola is an affectionate name for an indigenous Andean girl or woman.

La Chola was, during the late twentieth century, a popular Cusco *chichería*, a pub in which one could drink *chicha*, a fermented corn beverage, and eat typical Andean food.

BARADIEL CARGANDO CON PÓLVORA SU ARCABÚS

Decoratión mural
Capilla de Sangarará

Soy el arcángel apócrifo

Soy el paria al que los legos llaman
Angel y príncipe del granizo

Oculto en la penumbra del sotacoro
en el fasto luneto de una cúpula
colmo mi ruedo: fronda tiznada
por el humo de los cirios

       No hay
más escenario: un árbol
un poco de tierra para asentar los pies
son el único paisaje circundante

Botas romanas, faldellín
capa volante

sobre mi escudo rige
un tordo ermitaño

No pertenezco a la jerarquía celeste
al enjambre de querubines, tronos, potencias
pulsando un laúd, violas
de gamba: *pura*
decoración pompeyana

Soy el bastardo sin linaje
En su lengua los feligreses
corrompieron mi nombre
proscrito

Anónimo, cerril
me recuesto en los gramales

BARADIEL LOADING GUNPOWDER INTO HIS HARQUEBUS

Wall vignette

Chapel of Sangarará

I am the apocryphal archangel

I am the pariah whom the lay folk call
Angel-prince of hail

Hidden in the dim chamber below the choir
in the ornate lunette of a cupola
I spill over my nook: a leaf covered with soot
from the smoke of the candles

> *There is not much*
landscape here: a tree
just enough land on which to stand
this is the only ground allotted him

Roman boots, short tunic
flowing cape

a hermit thrush
commands my coat of arms

I do not belong to the heavenly hierarchy
to the angelic choirs of cherubs, thrones, powers
who play their lutes or violas
da gamba: *simply*
embellishments in the Pompeian style

I am the bastard bereft of my heritage
In their language the parishioners
mispronounced
my outlawed name

Anonymous, unbroken
I recline in the soft grass

cansado al atardecer
como un peón que durante el día
                              pisó
pisoteó barro crudo
para el adobe

Soy el arcángel apócrifo

Soy el paria al que los legos llaman
Angel y príncipe del granizo

weary in the late afternoon
like the laborer who all day long
                                        stamped
and stamped again the loads of clay
for brick making

I am the apocryphal archangel

I am the pariah whom the lay folk call
Angel-prince of hail

NOTES

Baradiel is an obscure angel-prince mentioned in the Book of Enoch, a non-canonical scripture.

Sangarará is a small village located in the Cusco region. Sangarará was the site of a battle fought in 1780 between indigenous rebel forces led by Túpac Amaru II against the Spanish Colonial army. Túpac Amaru II's rebels triumphed in this battle.

LA ADÚLTERA
Óleo de BERNABÉ NINA
Genemuiden Museum, Netherlands

Alta al mediodía
como el rojo pendón que se yergue
en la puerta de las chicherías

Lejanías brumosas
¿rinconada de Maras?
¿de Poroy?

Abundosas carnaciones
El tul que ciñe
corpulencia de plebeya

¿los anatomistas
de Florencia?

Hay rompimiento de gloria
y amplio paisaje
rural

El encarne de su frente: piedra lisa
piedra lumbre
donde las moscas
resbalan

Gordos angelillos volantes
portan una cartela:

Dios te salve, María
Janny

Virgen del Lunar / La Peregrina

Madona de las Frutas
en actitud orante

THE FALLEN WOMAN
Oil by BERNABÉ NINA
Genemuiden Museum, Netherlands

A tall woman at noon
like the red pennant that flies
over the doors of the *chicherías*

A misty background
The threshold of Maras?
       of Poroy?

Voluptuous, fleshly
Her gauzy dress is snug
her figure corpulent and plebian

         Florentine
         anatomists?

A break in the heavens
and the vast landscape
         of the countryside

Her fleshy brow: a slippery stone
         a slick chunk of alum
on which flies
slide

Chubby little angels hover
carry a banner:

       May God save you, Maria
       Janny

Virgin of the Birthmark/The Wanderer

Madonna of the Ripe Fruit
in a posture of prayer

Virgen-Niña que se gestó
en la resonante barriga
de un arpa:

¿La Gran Ramera
de Babilonia?

(tu tedio guarda, vil
        odalisca,
el camposanto que discurre
a tus espaldas)

Virgin-Child who was nurtured
in the melodious belly
of a harp:

      The Whore
      of Babylon?

(your bored pose obscures,
         vile concubine,
the churchyard that stretches out
behind your back)

NOTES

Bernabé Nina was a School of Cusco painter who was born in the village of Huambutío in the Sacred Valley. Nina, who lived during the late seventeenth and early eighteenth centuries, was an immediate follower of Diego Quispe Tito, the greatest of the indigenous painters of the School of Cusco.

A *chichería* is a tavern that serves *chicha,* a popular Andean beverage made from fermented corn. A red banner traditionally indicates that fresh *chicha* is available at the tavern.

Poroy and *Maras* are villages in the Sacred Valley of Peru.

Janny is a contemporary woman's name.

SAN ISIDRO LABRADOR
BASILIO SANTA CRUZ PUMAQALLO
Catedral de Cusco

El lucero del amanecer
clarea en el firmamento
                                    brilla
como el ataúd de un párvulo
en un camposanto remoto:

            posible
constelación del arado

gran serenidad
casi estatismo

En el andén de las aves coloradas
los pájaros parlantes vaticinan lluvia
tormentas de granizo
                        ¿zaguán del cielo?

Isidro el labrador
no está en su puesto, y el dueño
de las parcelas de tierra
de los plantíos de coca
descubre que en su ausencia
los ángeles aran sus campos

                        (el fondo
se resuelve
en una floresta y
lejanías de rocas)

                    Por lo demás,
            de tanto trajinar tras los bueyes
            abriendo surcos en tierra y pedregales
            adquirí el mayor de mis males, viejo
            insomne:

SAINT ISIDORE THE FARMER
BASILIO SANTA CRUZ PUMAQALLO
Cathedral of Cusco

The morning star
begins to brighten in the firmament
                                        it shines
like the white coffin of a child
in a distant churchyard:

  suggesting
the constellation of the plow

a great serenity
a motionless calm

On the terrace crowded with red parrots
chattering birds predict rain
and hailstorms
                        could this be the path of heaven?

Isidore the farmer
is not at his post, and the owner
of these parcels of land
planted with coca
discovers that in his absence
the angels are plowing his fields

                        (the background
dissolves
into an arbor and
a far-off field of boulders)

                A few things more,
                as the oxen traveled back and forth
                driving furrows into the rocky ground
                I acquired the greatest of my misfortunes, old
                weary laborer that I am:

tengo
arenilla acumulada en los riñones
y mis aperos de labranza, los yugos
reposan
en el solar de San Eladio
patrono de los herreros

now I have
stones forming in my kidneys
and my hoe and harrow, the yoke for my beasts
rest
on the plot of St. Eligius
patron of blacksmiths

NOTES

Basilio Santa Cruz Pumaqallo was a master of the School of Cusco. He painted *Saint Isidore the Farmer* from 1691-1693.

Path of Heaven or *Zaguán del Cielo* is a narrow street in Cusco.

DESCENDIMIENTO DE LA VIRGEN
EN SUNTURWASI
Alegoría
MARCOS SAPAKA

Pintar a las desgranadoras de maíz
a las vivanderas del Portal de Panes
era mi mayor deseo

Pinté
a la Virgen María embarazada
y me llamaron pactario

algunos cuadros son recreaciones
de evangelios apócrifos

En mi fresco
La divina pastora de las almas
   —con censura eclesiástica—
abundosos pechos de nodriza, la Virgen de las Mercedes
da de lactar de un seno
al Niño-Dios su hijo, y del otro
a San Pedro Nolasco, patrón
de la Orden Mercedaria

el lienzo
es impío y de mano
indígena

En el *Cristo caído*
después de la flagelación
no hay detalles
no amorcillos:

el paño del pudor
         apenas
si cubre los genitales

DESCENT OF THE VIRGIN TO
THE SUNTURWASI
An Allegory
MARCOS SAPAKA

To paint the threshers of corn
and the women who cook at the Bread Entrance
was my greatest wish

           I painted
the pregnant Virgin Mary
and they accused me of being a spell caster

some paintings are recreations
of apocryphal gospels

In my fresco
The Divine Shepherdess of Souls
    —roundly condemned by the Church—
the Virgin of the Mercies, her breasts as full as those of a wet nurse
gives one breast
to the Son of God her child, and the other
to Saint Peter Nolasco, patron
of the Mercedarian Order

                    this canvas
                    is profane and from the hand
                    of an indigenous painter

In the *Fallen Christ*
after the Flagellation
there are no embellishments
no cherubs in flight

a loincloth
          scarcely
covers the genitals

del Rey de Reyes:
                        una copia
de los grabados de Wierix o van Tulden

Con él
hay una incorporación de flora y fauna
propias de estas tierras

Son, además,
telas de mis obrajes:

El cantar de los cantares, colección particular
La comunión del asno, de paradero desconocido
San Francisco revolcándose desnudo
en la nieve,
                        tres veces
repintada y cubierta
con follajería ficticia

of the King of Kings:
                    a copy
of an engraving by Wierix or van Tulden

This artist often
incorporates native flora and fauna
in his work

I produced, besides
other works:

The Song of Songs, now in a private collection
The Donkey's Communion, whereabouts unknown
St. Francis Tumbling down Naked
in the Snow
                    this last one
repainted and covered three times
with foliage that was foreign to me

NOTES

The *sunturwasi* was an Inca military building used for storing arms and military emblems. The Virgin Mary was said to have visited the site of the sunturwasi of Cusco. Later the Spaniards erected a church, El Triunfo, over the remains of the original Inca building. The sunturwasi was the site of an unsuccessful revolt led by the Inca Manco in 1536 against the Spaniards.

Marcos Sapaka (sometimes spelled Sapaca or Zapata) was active during the eighteenth century and painted some 200 religious works. His work often mixes the sacred and the profane.

The Bread Entrance or *Portal de Panes* is one of the principal entrances to the main square of Cusco. It was originally the site of the residence of the Inca Pachacutec.

Anton Wierix II was a sixteenth-century Flemish engraver known for his religious subjects. *Theodoor van Tulden* (or Thulden) was a seventeenth-century Flemish painter and engraver.

EL PINTOR/Los Artificios
Dibujo de FELIPE GUAMÁN POMA
Nueva Corónica y Buen Gobierno

Soy el Anónimo de Juli, de Quito, de Calamarca...

Yo que fui capaz de humectar
el leve bisel de los labios
de la *Virgen-Niña hilando*

de develar los ojos acuosos
de la *Magdalena penitente*
                        los pies
de San Cristóbal en el agua
pisando bancos de peces
                        y retocar
sin fin
las carnaduras róseas
de las manos del *Ángel*
portando una cesta de pan
                        no pude
dibujar
las letras de mi propio nombre
y apellido

              Los pintureros
                        no saben
              firmar leer ni escribir
              Por ellos lo hacen a ruego
                    los plumarios
              calígrafos diestros en el uso
              de la pluma de escribir

Soy el Anónimo de La Almudena,
de Santa Clara, de Nazarenas,
de la capilla de Huarocondo...

THE PAINTER/His Early Works
A Sketch by FELIPE GUAMÁN POMA
New Chronicle and Good Government

I am the Anonymous One of Juli, Quito, Calamarca...

I was able to moisten
the slight bevel of the lips
of *The Young Virgin at Her Spinning Wheel*

to reveal the watery eyes
of *The Penitent Magdalene*
                 the feet
of Saint Christopher in the water
stamping on shoals of fish
                 who could retouch
endlessly
the rosy skin
of the hands of the *Angel*
Carrying a Basket of Bread
                 but I could not
form
the letters of my own first
and last names

           These artisans
                 did not know
           how to sign their own names or read or write
           For that reason they had to plead
              with scribes,
           those skilled in the use
           of the writer's quill

I am the Anonymous One of The Almudena Church,
of Santa Clara, The Nazarenes,
of the Chapel of Huarocondo...

NOTES

New Chronicle and Good Government (1615) was a book written by the indigenous writer Felipe Guamán Poma to provide the Spanish king both with the history of pre-conquest Peru and to describe the destructive effects of colonization on Peruvian native society. Guamán Poma was also an accomplished fine artist who specialized in paintings of the Virgin Mary; his paintings, however, are not well known.

ADORACIÓN DE LOS PASTORES
Escena galante
FRANCISCO CHIWANTITO

Una maraña de nubes cubre
la constelación del colibrí

de la tropilla de llamas
                en celo

En el pesebre ¿tambo de Rayampata?
cunde la quietud, la tensa calma
que precede a un combate
a una tormenta

                        adopción
              de poses muelles y reposadas

Sobre un pellejo de cabra
el Niño-Dios retoza
desnudo:

              ¿… y estito?
                        indagan

los troperos de Lucre, los sendeadores
los llameros de la nación Paruro
los arrieros de la pampa de Anta
los leñateros, las hilanderas
los salineros de Maras

El Buen Pastor carga
un corderillo, y el conjunto
es guiado por un ángel
con la trompeta de la predicación

En la canasta de retama
los Reyes Magos han dejado

ADORATION OF THE SHEPHERDS
A Pastoral Scene
FRANCISCO CHIWANTITO

A thicket of clouds covers
the constellations of the hummingbird

and the flock of llamas
  in heat

In the manger...the cave of Rayampata?
a tense calm extends, like the stillness
that comes before a battle
or a storm

> *figures*
> *in softened and relaxed postures*

On a goatskin pelt
the God-Child wiggles in delight
naked:

> ... and who is this little one?
> > inquire

the cowherders from Lucre, the trekkers
the llama herders from the Paruro nation
the drovers from the plains of Anta
the wood cutters, the women who spin wool
the salt miners from Maras

The Good Shepherd cradles
a little lamb, and the group
is guided by an angel
with a herald's trumpet

In the reed basket
the Kings of Orient have left

jenjibre de Malabar, sándalo de Timor
clavo de Molucas, alcanfor de Borneo
canela de Ceylan

La Virgen
el Niño y los ángeles lucen
esa belleza dulce y boba:

uno de los encantos
de la pintura cusqueña

Cordero de Dios
Hijo del Hombre
el recién nacido tiene
dos remolinos en la testa:
                         señal
de que será obstinado

ginger from Malabar, sandalwood from Timor
cloves from the Moluccas, camphor from Borneo
cinnamon from Ceylon

>*The Virgin*
>*the Child and the angels glow*
>*with a sweet and simple beauty:*
>
>*one of the delights*
>*of Cusqueñan art*

Lamb of God
Son of Man
the newborn has
two whorls in his hair:
                    the mark
of one who will be stubborn

NOTES

Francisco Chiwantito was a prolific indigenous painter of the Cusco School, active
mostly during the latter part of the seventeenth century. He was best known for his
detailed depictions of landscapes and scenes of monastic life.

Rayampata, Lucre, Paruro, Anta, and *Maras* are villages in the Cusco region.

LA EXPULSIÓN DEL PARAÍSO
Boceto
TALLER DEL MAESTRO DE ACOMAYO

Flotan las primeras manchas ¿Aparición de la Virgen?
Y los doctrineros acechan / me rondan
¿Los mártires franciscanos del Japón?
El ángel con la trompeta de la predicación

> *Al dicho Gremio de Pintores*
> *se le exige y demanda pintar*
> *únicamente lo que dicen las Escrituras*
> *so pena de excomunión*

Acólitos, diáconos, tonsurados
presbíteros, hostiarios y lectores
me vigilan como a un reo
                          en vano
me inculcan ochenta veces al día
el mismo pasaje del evangelio
                cristiano

                        ¿resultados?

Adán y Eva
llevan el peso de la composición
pero el Edén abunda en árboles
                de kiswar
hordas de loros y flores de ñukchu

> *Idos, impíos*
> *Salíos del reino*

Detrás de la pareja abatida
una tropilla de llamas apacenta
en la hoyada de Mawayani

        ¿carneros de Indias?

THE EXPULSION FROM PARADISE
A Study
THE STUDIO OF THE MASTER OF ACOMAYO

The first pigments float on the canvas. The apparition of the Virgin?
The zealots keep a sharp eye out / they prowl around me
The Franciscan martyrs of Japan?
The herald angel with his trumpet

> *To the Guild of Painters*
> *we hereby command you may paint*
> *only what the Scriptures say*
> *under the penalty of excommunication*

Acolytes, deacons, tonsured monks
priests, thurifers and lectors
watch over me as one would watch a criminal

                                                    in vain

they drum into me eighty times a day
the same passage from the gospel
          of Christ

                              and the result?

Adam and Eve
carry the weight of the composition
but this Eden abounds
          in kiswar trees
hordes of parrots and ñukchu flowers

> *Be gone, ye impious ones*
> *Depart ye from the kingdom*

Behind the woeful couple
a flock of llamas grazes
in the gully of Mawayani

          lambs of the Indies?

En la copa del Arbol Prohibido
¿lúcumo
          chirimoya?
anida una wallata
o ganso de los Andes

In the crown of the Forbidden Tree
A lúcumo?
        a cherimoya?
nests a wallata
or goose of the Andes

NOTES

The Master of Acomayo was an anonymous colonial-era indigenous painter from the village of Acomayo, located near Cusco.

The Franciscan Martyrs of Japan were a group of Franciscan priests and hundreds of early Japanese converts killed in 1622 by the shogun of Japan, who sought to abolish Christianity.

The *kiswar* tree is a tree native to Peru.

The *ñukchu* is a flower native to the Cusco region.

The *lúcumo* (also called *lucmo*) and *cherimoya* (also called the custard apple) are fruit-bearing trees native to Peru.

The *wallata* or *goose of the Andes* is a species of goose native to Peru.

RETRATO DE DON MANUEL MOLLINEDO Y AN-GULO OBISPO DEL CUSCO
CÍRCULO DE QUISPE TITO
Iglesia de San Sebastián

Vine a las Indias: pastor de almas
con estudios y aguadas de El Greco
con dos arcángeles de Zurbarán
                  y grabados
de los maestros holandeses

La composición de su ropaje
rojo cardenal / rojo de Tiziano
          requirió
setenta capas de bermellones

        No fui yo
quien prohibió la representación de desnudos
de la Virgen, de los profetas:

                  fue
el Concilio de Trento / el Concilio Limense

De los cuadros vetados, arrumados
          para el fuego
rescaté muchos:

Santa Teresa traspasada por el dardo del Angel
Salomé con la cabeza del Bautista
San Antonio tentado por dos diablesas, y
          aquél otro
en el que, en la mazmorra de los cristianos,
una ramera da de lactar a su padre
sediento y moribundo

La oxidación de los barnices apenas
si permite intuir

PORTRAIT OF DON MANUEL MOLLINEDO Y AN-GULO BISHOP OF CUSCO
CIRCLE OF QUISPE TITO
Church of Saint Sebastian

I came to the Indies: a shepherd of souls
with sketches and watercolors by El Greco
with two archangels by Zurbarán
                             and engravings
by the Dutch Masters

The color of his vestments
cardinal red/Titian red
                required
seventy coats of vermillion

        I was not the one
who forbade the nude representations
of the Virgin, of the prophets:

                         it was
The Council of Trent/The Council of Lima

Of the paintings that were banned, piled in a heap
                     to be burned
I rescued many:

Saint Teresa Pierced by the Angel's Arrow
Salome with the Head of John the Baptist
Saint Anthony Tested by Two She-Demons, and
                 another work
in which, deep in a dungeon filled with Christians,
a harlot suckled her father
who was parched and dying

The oxidation of the glaze barely
allows one to discern

el color original: rostro cetrino
la negra semilla de los ojos
en arrobamiento místico

La corona condal
el escudo de armas de mi linaje
perduran grabados
en la campana de una capilla
perdida en los Andes:

¿Cai-Cai, Zurite, Urquillos?

Vine a las Indias: pastor de almas
                    vicario
de exercicio pintor:

          "Desde su cruz
el amor sopla su aliento divino
al alma crucificada
                    y le infunde
la vida del espíritu"

the original color: sallow face
the black pupils
swept up in mystic rapture

My family crest
our hereditary coat of arms
still abides engraved
on a bell in a chapel
lost in the Andes:

Cai-Cai, Zurite, Urquillos?

I came to the Indies: a shepherd of souls
            a vicar
a patron of the arts:

  "From His cross
love blows His divine breath
into the crucified soul
               and instills in him
the life of the Spirit"

NOTES

The anonymous painter of this work was one of many painters influenced by Diego Quispe Tito, the great seventeenth-century indigenous painter of the School of Cusco.

Manuel de Mollinedo y Angulo was sent by Spain to administer religious life in Cusco. He arrived in 1673, bringing with him an important collection of art. Mollinedo came from a wealthy family, and he personally financed or induced others to finance the construction of scores of churches and works of religious art. Most of the artists who worked for Mollinedo were indigenous or mestizo artists.

Cai-Cai, Zurite, and *Urquillos* are all villages in Peru's Sacred Valley in the Cusco region.

LOS APRENDICES

Museo Santa Teresa, Ciudad de Arequipa

Creación de la mujer

El pudor de los monjes de este convento
hizo cubrir los senos de Eva
con tres capas de estuco

Jesús duerme en la tempestad

La firma del autor yace
                    oculta
en el reverso del lienzo
en una cinta que cuelga
del pico de un pájaro:

¿wanchaco
                zorzal
calandria?

El pecado original

Está dañado por goteras
                        y tiene
desprendimiento de la capa
                pictórica

Escenas del evangelio

La serie de profetas, sibilas y padres
                    de la iglesia
es obra de círculo de imitadores:

responde a una motivación
claramente tenebrista

APPRENTICE PAINTERS
Saint Theresa Museum, City of Arequipa

The Creation of Woman

The prudishness of the monks of this monastery
required that Eve's breasts be covered
with three layers of plaster

Jesus Asleep in the Storm

The signature of the artist lies
                    hidden
on the back of the canvas
in a ribbon that hangs
from the beak of a bird:

a wanchaco?
            a zorzal?
a calandria?

Original Sin

This is being ruined by a leaky roof
                        and it has
a detached layer
        of paint

Scenes from the Gospels

The series of prophets, sibyls and fathers
                of the Church
is the work of a circle of imitators:

it reflects a motivation
that is clearly tenebrist

La parábola del sembrador

El paisaje urbano que se ve
           al fondo
detrás de San Crispín
           y San Crispiniano
patronos del gremio de zapateros
es Huamanga

El martirio de San Laureano

La composición no es original
fue tomada de un grabado holandés
del siglo XVIII

hay vacíos en grandes paños

The Parable of the Sower

The urban setting that one sees
                in the background
behind Saint Crispin
                and Saint Crispinian
patrons of the guild of shoemakers
is Huamanga

The Martyrdom of Saint Laureano

The composition is not original
it was taken from a Dutch engraving
from the XVIII century

there are large gaps in its panels

NOTES

The *wanchaco* or *huanchaco* is a black and red bird.

The *zorzal* is a songbird of the thrush family.

The *calandria* is type of mockingbird.

These three birds are native to Peru.

Huamanga is a city in the Ayacucho region.

Museo de Indias
The Museum of the Indies

En uno de los cruceros, hay una tela digna de figurar en cualquier museo

In one of the transepts, there is a canvas worthy of display in any museum

—Felipe Cossio del Pomar

DIOS MUESTRA EL PARAÍSO A ADÁN Y EVA
18th Century
CUSCO SCHOOL
The Metropolitan Museum of Art, New York

Bosque de Colcampata
                        Ceja de selva
¿Frutales de la hacienda Urco?
¿Fundo Manzanares?

Las carnaciones de Eva, holgadas
rebasan los ojos del buey
primero

Una brizna cubre su sexo ¿ramita de toronjil?

Hay, al menos treinta tipos de pájaros
dispersos en la vegetación

La flor del paraíso / flor de la granadilla
                                 retoña
verde nilo
             rojo bandera
en los claros del bosque

Y salía un río de Edén
que regaba el huerto

                      Plantaciones ¿de té?

¿cafetales de fundos agrícolas?
Un ternero de los centros de engorde
no naturaleza muerta
                    un
graffiti:

salida a la derecha

GOD SHOWS PARADISE TO ADAM AND EVE
18th Century
CUSCO SCHOOL
The Metropolitan Museum of Art, New York

The forest of Colcampata
                    Eyebrow of the rainforest
The orchards of the Urco hacienda?
The Manzanares Estate?

Eve's naked charm, voluptuous flesh
the sleepy eyes of the first ox
cannot take it all in

A slender leaf covers her sex…a sprig of lemon balm?

Here, at least thirty types of birds
are scattered in the vegetation

The bird of paradise/the passion fruit blossom
                                        sprouts
Nile green
                flag red
in the forest clearing

And a river went out of Eden
that watered the garden

                    Tea plantations?

Coffee haciendas?
The lowing of cattle at the troughs
No still life
        one
graffito:

exit on the right

dos ángeles turiferarios sahuman
las preñeces de María

¿madre tierra?

Hortus conclusus / huerto cerrado

two thurifer angels perfume
the last months of Mary's pregnancy

Mother Earth?

Hortus conclusus/cloistered garden

NOTES

Colcampata is an Inca palace located in the northern part of Cusco. In the sixteenth century, the Spanish conquerors gave the palace of Colcampata to Cristobal Paullu Inca, one of the puppet Incas installed by the Spanish.

Urco, a small village in Peru's Sacred Valley, was the home of Inca Urco, one of the sons of the emperor Viracocha Inca, who ruled during the early fifteenth century.

Manzanares is a hacienda in Calca, a town in Peru's Sacred Valley.

EL HIJO PRÓDIGO

Iglesia de San Sebastián

Antes de pintar *La dormición de la Virgen*
las parábolas o la serie
de ángeles arcabuceros, mis manos
desgranaban maíz
en los tendales del Corregidor

> *ningún pintor cusqueño*
> *empequeñece tanto sus personajes*
> *en aras del paisaje*

En la calle Mantas / Cuesta del Alabado
en el taller del maestro italiano
Bernardo Demócrito Bitti, aprendí
el efecto de distancias, las perspectivas
de engaño y los rompimientos de gloria

El gran Zurbarán — en su etapa tenebrista —
me enseñó la técnica de la luz de cueva:

entrando por la parte superior del cuadro
la luz incide sobre los lados visibles
de las personas y los objetos
dejando el resto sumergido
en las tinieblas

> *en sus cuadros, Cristo*
> *flota en la cruz*

Digamos que no todo
se fraguó sobre tela / también
he pintado en los netos de las naves
de la Catedral del Cusco,
                    en las arcadas

THE PRODIGAL SON

Church of Saint Sebastian

Before painting *The Dormition of the Virgin*
the parables or the series
of angels armed with harquebuses, my hands
were shelling corn
in the sheds of the Landowner

> *no other painter in Cusco*
> *so diminishes his subjects*
> *in deference to the landscape*

In the Street of Blankets / Hill of Praise
in the studio of the Italian master
Bernardo Demócrito Bitti, I learned
the effect of distances, how to frame perspective
how to open the heavens

The master Zurbarán — in his tenebrist period —
taught me the technique of cave lighting:

streaming in from the top part of the painting
the light falls on the visible surfaces
of the people and objects
leaving everything else submerged
in shadows

> *in his paintings, Christ*
> *floats on the cross*

I have to say that I did not
labor solely on canvas / I have also
painted in the ambries of the naves
of Cusco's Cathedral,
> in the archways

de la capilla
de mi pueblo natal

En los brazos del transepto de La Compañía
El arcángel Rafael pintado
en la pechina del arco de un templete
lleva el pescado con cuya hiel
curará la ceguera de Tobías
santo y mártir
del secreto de confesión

el maestro
hacía el trazo general del cuadro
limitándose a cara y manos

uno de los discípulos ponía
la mancha principal de color, otro
las florestas y otro las aves
y el conjunto se acababa
con la aplicación del brocateado:
oro superpuesto en plantilla
sobre halos, vestidos y cortinajes

Las sombras se logran con bases
de tierra sena y huesos calcinados

La cochinilla o grana de México tiñe
de rojo indio / aunque
también se obtiene del achiote
y del árbol *sangre de drago*

Del nogal salen los tonos ocres / el bol
de Armenia es la arcilla rojo-teja

todo esto después se enluce
con la hiel de los porcinos

of the chapel
of my hometown

In the branches of the transept of the Compañía Church
I painted *The Archangel Raphael*
in the concha of the canopy arch
he carries the fish with whose gall
he will cure the blindness of Tobias
saint and martyr
of the confidentiality of confession

> *the master*
> *used to make a general outline of the painting*
> *reserving for himself faces and hands*
>
> *one of his disciples filled in*
> *most of the pigment, another*
> *the woods, another the birds*
> *and the composition was finished*
> *with the application of the gilding:*
> *gold superimposed in a pattern*
> *over the halos, garments and drapery*

The shadings result from pigments
derived from rich soil and burnt bones

The cochineal or Mexican scarlet provides the tint
of Indian red/although
this color can also be obtained from the achiote
and from the *dragon blood tree*

From the walnut comes the ocher tones/the powder
of Armenia is the source of brick red

finally all this is glazed over
with the gall of young pigs

barroco indio
manierista andino / el pintor
que firmaba sus cuadros
con un pajarito:

> D. Diego Quispe Tito,
> de su mano y a su costa.

Indian baroque
Andean mannerist/the artist
who signed his paintings
with a little bird:

D. Diego Quispe Tito,
from his hands and his own money.

NOTES

Saint Sebastian is a neighborhood in Cusco.

The landowner (in Spanish, *corregidor*) was, during Peru's colonial period, a wealthy and powerful local authority who possessed much land and many servants.

Bernardo Demócrito Bitti (1548-1610) was an Italian-born Jesuit priest and painter sent to South America on a mission "to evangelize through art." In addition to producing his own canvases, Bitti taught painting to the indigenous people of Peru. He is largely responsible for initiating the artistic movement known as the School of Cusco.

The ornate *Cathedral of Cusco,* built by the Jesuits in the sixteenth and seventeenth centuries, is located on Cusco's main square, the Plaza de Armas.

The *Compañía Church* is a baroque church in Cusco's main square. It was built by the Jesuits in the sixteenth and seventeenth centuries and is located across from the Cathedral of Cusco.

Diego Quispe Tito (1611-1667) was the most famous and influential of the painters of the School of Cusco. The son of a noble Inca family, Diego Quispe Tito produced scores of outstanding religious paintings, many of which reveal the mannerist influence, then current in Europe. He is also known for his spacious landscapes, which often feature birds and angels.

ESTUDIOS DE ÁNGELES
ANÓNIMO
Tocuyo de Pitumarca

— Ángel gatillando su arcabús

— Arcángel con arma de fuego

— Ángel cargando con pólvora
   su arcabús

— Ángel en posición de disparar

LEYENDA

Vestidos para la guerra, los ángeles arcabuceros
— caras ovales ojos asirios — acampan aquí
entre los hombres de buena fe. Sus poses marciales
fueron tomadas del manual militar *El ejercicio
de las armas,* un libro de grabados del siglo XVII.

STUDIES OF ANGELS
ANONYMOUS
Pitumarca Canvas

—An angel cocking his harquebus

—An angel with a firearm

—An angel loading his harquebus
with gunpowder

—An angel poised to shoot

LEGEND

Dressed for war, these harquebusier angels
—oval faces and Assyrian eyes— encamp here
among the men of good faith. Their martial poses
were taken from the military manual *The Military
Drills of the Armed Forces*, a book of engravings
dating from the XVII century.

NOTES

Pitumarca is a village in Peru's Sacred Valley.

MATRIMONIO DE DON MARTÍN DE LOYOLA CON DOÑA BEATRIZ ÑUSTA

ANÓNIMO

Iglesia de La Compañía, Cusco

En el bisel de mis labios
tengo un lunar que jamás
       hallarán

(Menuda y sobria
la novia posa
             aquí
al centro
sin el pedestal
de los tacos altos)

Por siglos cuelga
bajo la bóveda coral de esta iglesia
mi ceremonia nupcial
con la farsa de un enlace imposible:

Con este matrimonio emparentaron entre sí
la real casa de los reyes Incas del Perú
con las dos casas de Loyola y Borja
Exmos Señores grandes de primera clase

Me casé
mientras mis tropas guerreaban en Vilcabamba
y porque mi padre había pactado y se hizo cristiano

       Un caso típico:
no hubo declaración de contrayentes
ni pregón de edictos
ni amonestaciones

En planos sucesivos
conforman el lienzo
tres grupos separados:
              el pintor

THE MARRIAGE OF DON MARTÍN DE LOYOLA AND DOÑA BEATRIZ ÑUSTA

ANONYMOUS

The Compañía Church, Cusco

On the bevel of my lip
I have a tiny birthmark that you will never
        discover

(Petite and serious
the bride poses
                here
in the middle
no high-heeled shoes
to raise her up)

For centuries it hangs
under the choir vault of this church
my nuptial ceremony
with its farce of an impossible union:

With this marriage are hereby joined as family
the royal house of the Inca kings of Peru
and the two houses of Loyola and Borja
their Excellencies being noble lords of the highest rank

I married
meanwhile my troops were skirmishing in Vilcabamba
and because my father had made a pact and converted to Christianity

        A typical case:
there was neither a declaration of consent
nor an official proclamation
nor banns of marriage

In distinct sections
the canvas incorporates
three separate groupings:
                the painter

no pudo
cómo juntar a sus personajes

Aquí estoy en minoría
                              Soy
del linaje imperial de Yucay

            Me subyuga
el parloteo de los loros

San Ignacio de Loyola y San Francisco de Borja
¿testigos de la boda?
piensan y viven en el lienzo

Vestido a la moda de los felipes
—sus manos tienen blancuras femeninas—
mi consorte galantea:
                              mas
no seré yo
la concubina que se ahorque
con sus trenzas

could not unite
his subjects

Here I am in the minority
                    I am
of the imperial lineage of Yucay

        The chatter of the parrots
transports me

Saint Ignacio de Loyola and San Francisco de Borja
witnesses to the wedding?
appear thoughtful and alive in the painting

Dressed in the style of the royals
—his hands a feminine shade of white—
my consort offers me a gesture of affection:
                                                    but

I will not be
the concubine who hangs herself
with her own braids

NOTES

A *ñusta* is an Inca princess.

The *Compañía Church* is a baroque church in Cusco's main square. It was built by the Jesuits in the sixteenth and seventeenth centuries.

Vilcabamba is a remote jungle city located about 100 miles from Cusco. It was the capital-in-exile of Manco Inca, who carried out a guerrilla war against the Spanish. Vilcabamba was sacked by the Spanish in 1572.

Yucay is located in Peru's Sacred Valley near Cusco. Yucay was home to a number of Incas, including the Inca Sauri Túpac, who was one of the rebels of Vilcabamba.

LAMENTACIÓN DE MARÍA
ANTE EL CADÁVER DE CRISTO
ANÓNIMO
Templo de Characato

La ausencia de pájaros
                    señala

que este lienzo tal vez
no fue pintado
en la muy noble y leal
ciudad del Cusco

LAMENTATION OF MARY
BEFORE THE BODY OF CHRIST
ANONYMOUS
Church of Characato

The absence of birds
                    suggests

that perhaps this canvas
was not painted
in the very noble and faithful
city of Cusco.

NOTES

Characato is a small village near the city of Arequipa.

LA PROCESIÓN DEL CORPUS
FRAGMENTO
Serie de 15 lienzos
Museo de Arte Religioso

Si el Cusco
  cabeza de los reinos del Perú
pereciera por un terremoto igual
  al de 1650
cada solar, calle o plaza
  sería reconstruido tal cual
siguiendo el recorrido procesional
  pintado en esta serie
1680. Plaza Mayor
  El pueblo en primer plano
Doblan las campanas
  Todo el valor de la obra está
en el tratamiento de masas
  Horas punta
¿No es la feria
  del Baratillo de los sábados?
Portal de Carnes y Calle Mantas
  un mar de gente
A los feligreses los une
  la cercanía de los pasajeros que viajan
inermes sobre sus bultos
  en un camión cargado al máximo:
Peso neto: 5000 kilos
  Plazuela de La Almudena
no extras no figurantes
  El Gremio de Plateros y los maestros doradores
los tintoreros de Langui-Layo
  los frazaderos de Maranganí
un tamborero y un rezador:
  ¿cabezas de estudio?
Cuesta de La Amargura / Callejón Violín
  Salgan muchachas a sus balcones
que los ciencianos han de pasar
  Un venerable de la orden mercedaria

THE PROCESSION OF THE CORPUS CHRISTI
FRAGMENT
Series of 15 canvases
Museum of Religious Art

If Cusco
   capital of the kingdom of Peru
should perish by an earthquake equal
   to the one of 1650
each manor house, street and city square
   would be rebuilt such as they appear
in the holy processional
   painted in this series
1680. Main Square
   The village folk in the foreground
The bells ring
   What is most significant about this work
is the depiction of the crowds
   Rush hour now
Isn't that the Saturday open-air market
   the one we call the Baratillo Fair?
The Livestock Entrance and the Street of Blankets
   a sea of people
The parishioners join together
   like travelers who journey
unarmed with their bundles
   in a wagon packed to capacity:
Net weight: 5000 kilos
   In the little plaza of the Almudena
no stragglers, no strangers
   The Guild of Silversmiths and the master goldsmiths
the dyers of Langui-Layo
   the blanket weavers of Maranganí
a drummer and a supplicant:
   studies of heads?
The Hill of Bitterness/Fiddle Alley
   Girls, come out on your balconies
the Ciencianos are about to pass by
   A venerable from the Mercedarian Order

El Inca Sayri Tupaq / un alférez indio
     no identificado
un músico trasnochado
     ¿el platillero de la banda Cazorla?
avanzan en la multitud:
     camionadas de silencio los separan
Arco de Santa Clara
     Portal Comercio y Desamparados:

Fatigaba el sol a los oyentes y llamó
     el Santo multitud de golondrinas
que entretejiendo sus alas
     les hicieron sombra

The Inca Sayri Tupaq / an Indian official
and a man whom no one really knows
   a musician who plays all night
     the cymbalist from the Cazorla band?
advance into the crowd:
    but container trucks of silence separate them
The Arch of Saint Claire
      The Entrance of Traders and Orphans Street:

The sun was wearying the listeners and the Saint
    called forth a multitude of swallows
who by interweaving their wings
    created shade for the parishioners

NOTES

The villages of *Langui* and *Layo* are located by Lake Languilayo in the vicinity of Cusco.

Maranganí is a community in the vicinity of Cusco and is located by the Vilcanota River.

The Hill of Bitterness and *Fiddle Alley* are narrow steep streets in Cusco.

Ciencianos are students from the Colegio de Ciencias, one of the oldest secondary schools in Cusco.

Inca Sayri Tupac (c. 1535-1561) ruled the independent Inca state of Vilcabamba for ten years and eventually was persuaded by the Spanish to convert to Catholicism. When Sayri Tupac was a child, the Spanish conquerors killed both his mother and father. Manco Inca Yupanqui, the father of Sayri Tupac, was the last ruling Inca emperor.

The *Cazorla band* was, during the twentieth century, the most well-known group of traditional Cusqueñan musicians.

EL PARAÍSO DE LA BÓVEDA BAÍDA
¿MURAL DEL PADRE SALAMANCA?
Capilla sin Nombre, Nave Derecha

Lazarillo de San Froylán
    / el pajarero
Pariente de San Blas, patrono
de los cargadores de bultos
        Soy
el monje mercedario, el asceta que tuvo
un *paraíso* pintado en la pared
      de su celda

      ¿es firmado
      o atribuído?

Ángeles instrumentalistas guardan
la desnudez de Eva
El Varón y su ancha espalda
      de batán

En la copa de la granadilla
árbol del bien / árbol del mal
        trina
un zorzal pata-amarilla
cerril pajarraco que desdeñado
por los de su propia especie
      anida
en la arenilla de los ríos, en los ortigales
en los puros espinos y abrojos

El pintor aporta
abundante ornamentación de follajes
volutas, guirnaldas y lambrequines

En la pilastra dórica / en las enjutas
      del arco
hay una serie de miniaturas alusivas

THE PARADISE OF THE VAULTED CEILING
MURAL BY THE SALAMANCA PRIEST?
Nameless Chapel, Right Nave

Guide of Saint Froylan
/ the keeper of birds
Relative of Saint Blaise, patron
of those who carry bundles
I am
the Mercedarian monk, the ascetic who had
a *paradise* painted on the wall
of his cell

is it signed
or attributed?

Harp-playing angels guard
Eve's nakedness
The Holy Man and his back broad
as a millstone

In the crown of the passion fruit tree
tree of good / tree of evil
trills
a yellow-legged zorzal
a wild hideous bird scorned
by those of its own species
nests
in the rocks alongside rivers, in beds of nettles
in the sharpest thorns and spines

The painter contributes
abundant ornamental foliage
flourishes, garlands and draperies

On the Doric pilaster / in the spandrels
between the arches
are a series of allusive miniatures

ODI GONZALES 65

a la vida de los Mártires del Colegio
de Agonizantes de San Camilo de Lelis

¿escuela veneciana?

Adyacente a la puerta del órgano
en el zócalo de mi celda pinté
        una versión india
de El cantar de los cantares:

Dime tú, amado de mi alma,
¿dónde pastoreas, dónde
sesteas al mediodía?

Paraíso de la bóveda baída
viñas, frutales, maizales,
trigales del quinto rapto
del beato Amadeo

that tell the story of the Dying Martyrs
of Saint Camillus of Lellis's Hospital

the Venetian School?

Adjacent to the door to the organ
on the baseboard of my cell wall I painted
        an Indian version
of the Song of Songs:

Tell me, beloved of my soul,
where do you pasture your flock, where
do you rest at noon?

Paradise of the vaulted ceiling
vineyards, orchards, cornfields
wheat fields of the fifth rapture
of the Blessed Amadeus.

NOTES

A monk of the Mercedarian order, *Friar Francisco Salamanca* was born in what is now Bolivia. He lived the last thirty years of his life as a hermit in his cell in the Convent of the Merced in Cusco and died in 1737. As a poet, he composed poems in Quechua and Aymara, but he was most well known for the frescoes he painted in his cell.

The *zorzal* is a songbird of the thrush family.

SUSANA Y LOS VIEJOS
Serie narrativa
ANTONIO SINCHI ROCA
Templo de Zurite

Acompañada de dos doncellas
entró Susana al jardín
para bañarse allí

¿van Dyck, Rubens?

!Enormes gordas y sos hogueras!

     Yo

soy capaz de reconocer a ellas
por el flujo / por el caudal de sus aguas
        menores

pero a ella
tras cortinas o matorrales
la distinguiría en sí
por el bullir de la riada
por el torrente
de los chorros finales

No había nadie allí
excepto los viejos que la espiaban
        ocultos
a la hora del baño

        ¿Fermín
Apolonio?

    pícaros vejetes
con avidez de lactantes

SUZANNA AND THE ELDERS
Narrative series
ANTONIO SINCHI ROCA
Zurite Church

Accompanied by two maid servants
Suzanna entered the garden
to bathe there

Van Dyck? Rubens?

Enormous fat ladies and their inner bonfires!

     I myself

am able to recognize them
by their flow / by the way they pass
       their water

but as for her
behind drapes or a screen of shrubbery
I would distinguish her
by the turbulence of her stream
by the torrent
of the final spurts

No one was there
except the elders who were spying on her
      hidden
during her bathing time

          Fermin?
Apollonius?

  crafty old codgers
thirsty as nursing babies

SUSANA
ACOSADA POR LOS VIEJOS

grandiosa, pesada
como un camión carguero

"tiene cuatro varas de ancho
por cinco de alto"

SUSANA
ACUSADA POR LOS VIEJOS

¿Melchor, Venancio?

entonces los impíos

mandaron que se desnudara
para saciarse de su hermosura

Susana
perniles de torete

su vientre:
                declive
de los resbaladeros

SUZANNA
HARRASSED BY THE ELDERS

a big woman, heavy
as a packed wagon

"four yards wide
and five high"

SUZANNA
ACCUSED BY THE ELDERS

Melchor, Venancio?

then the impious ones

ordered her to uncover her nakedness
so that they might sate themselves with her beauty

Suzanna
haunches of a young bull

her belly:
slope
of slippery rocks

NOTES

Antonio Sinchi Roca, a descendant of Inca nobility, was a School of Cusco painter active during the seventeenth century.

MARÍA UNGE LOS PIES DE JESÚS

Antiguo Hospital de Naturales
Templo de Belén, Cajamarca

Una zariguella nuca-roja
venida del otro lado de los mares
           te sobrevuela

Compresas de arcilla, tablillas,
hojas de malva
para el dolor
de tus tobillos

agua de pétalos
para tu frente febril
hijo mío

El brocateado siempre
es planiforme: llena
las superficies de los ropajes
sin tomar en cuenta el plegado
de las vestiduras:

—capa pluvial / paños
 volantes de María

Bajo la luna llena
en el yermo desierto
¿valle de los volcanes
           de Andagua?
Jesús ayuna / ¿escuela
           de Quito?

Y en los abras y yerbazales
a solas recibiste
el salivazo de los rumiantes
el aguardiente puro
de los tratantes de ganado

MARY ANOINTS THE FEET OF JESUS

Ancient Hospital for Native Peoples
Church of Bethlehem, Cajamarca

A red-breasted flicker
blown from the other side of the sea
   flies over you

Compresses of clay, splints
malva leaves
for the pain
in your ankles

a soothing herbal tea
for your fevered brow
my son

The garments' textures are always
flat: the surfaces of the robes
are filled in
they do not reflect the folds
of the clothing:

—priestly cope/Mary's garments
fluttering

Under the full moon
in the lonely desert
the valley of the volcanoes
 of Andagua?
Jesus fasts / School
 of Quito?

And in the mountain passes and pastures
you were treated
to the spit of the ruminants
the strong brandy
of the livestock traders

Estirpe de pajareros
no raza de víboras
entre nosotros, hijo,
se acumularon
                    ¿lo ves?
camionadas de silencio

Descendents of bird keepers
not a race of serpents
between us, son,
they gathered
                could you see?
wagonloads of silence

NOTES

Andagua is located in southern Peru. It is known as the Valley of Volcanoes.

The Quito School was an artistic movement. In Quito, as in Cusco, painter-priests taught painting to indigenous and mestizo artists during the colonial period. The artists of the School of Quito produced impressive works, though in a different style from the School of Cusco artists.

ESCRITORES NARRAN LA VIDA Y HECHOS DE SANTA CATALINA DE SIENA
Oil on Canvas/Cusco Circle
Stern/Davis Collection

—Obra temprana del maestro de Pomata:
   su paleta fría de pincelada lamida
   y contornos definidos

—El lienzo tuvo cuatro repintes sucesivos
   por discípulos y aprendices

—Tiene un acentuado carácter flamenco

—El cuadro fue pintado con el mecenazgo
   de un minero de Potosí

—La estructura de la escena
   se desarrolla en profundidad
   con el punto de fuga
   discretamente hacia abajo

—La expresión facial es claramente bitesco
   el plegado de paños
   zurbaranesco

—Celajes en tonalidades rojizas

—Este lienzo fue sustraído
   de la capilla de Maca

WRITERS RECOUNT THE LIFE AND DEEDS OF SAINT CATHERINE OF SIENA
Oil On Canvas/Cusco Circle
Stern/Davis Collection

—Early work by the master of Pomata:
his cool palette marked by thin brushwork
and definite outlines

—The canvas was repainted four times in succession
by disciples and apprentices

—It has a pronounced Flemish style

—The picture was painted through the patronage
of a miner from Potosí

—The composition of the scene
acquires a sense of depth
because the vanishing point
is cleverly placed toward the bottom

—The facial expression is clearly after Bitti
the drape of the garments
is after Zurbarán

—Wisps of cloud in rosy shades

—This canvas was stolen
from the Chapel of Maca

NOTES

The *Master of Pomata* was an anonymous painter from the village of Pomata, located along the shore of Lake Titicaca.

Potosí is a city in Bolivia known for its silver mines.

Bernardo Democrito Bitti (1548-1610) was an Italian-born Jesuit priest and painter sent to South America on a mission "to evangelize through art." In addition to producing his own canvases, Bitti taught painting to the indigenous people of Peru. He is largely responsible for initiating the artistic movement known as the School of Cusco.

Maca is a village in Peru's Colca Canyon, near the city of Arequipa.

LA SIXTINA DE AMERICA
The Sistine Chapel of America

*El templo de Andahuaylillas, más conocido como
La Sixtina de América, alberga en su interior la
obra maestra de la pintura mural andina*

—Folleto turístico

*The Church of Andahuaylillas, better known as the
Sistine Chapel of America, houses in its interior
the masterpiece of Andean mural painting*

—Tourist brochure

EL TALLER DE NAZARETH
ANÓNIMO

Éste es, Señor,
el último de mis hijos,
el que llevará mi bastón
cuando ya no pueda más
de puro viejo

Templo de Calca / el Taller
de Nazareth

En el sfumato leonardesco
/brillo desmayado/
el Hijo del Carpintero empieza a dar
los primeros pasos:

Este país
es para ingenieros, terco desgraciado
Estudia, lucha por llevarte un pan
a la boca
(si es con mantequilla, mejor)
Entonces haz caso o ya verás,
saludos,
tu padre

El lienzo entero respira
un resabio medieval:
cielo
decorativo

El vástago no heredó el oficio paterno
¿mea culpa?
En el raso taller
jardín de la infancia
el párvulo silabea
la lengua materna

THE WORKSHOP OF NAZARETH
ANONYMOUS

This is, Lord,
the last of my sons,
the one who will carry my cane
when I am no longer able
because of old age

Church of Calca / The Workshop
of Nazareth

In the da Vincian sfumato
  /faded highlights/
the Carpenter's Son begins to take
his first steps:

This country
is for engineers, thwarted mulish boy
Study, struggle to bring a morsel of bread
          to your mouth
(if it's buttered, so much the better)
So pay attention or you'll see,
          regards,
                    your father

The whole canvas gives off
a medieval fustiness:
          decorated
            sky

The offspring did not inherit the paternal trade
                    mea culpa?
In the spare workshop
              a nursery school
the little one mouths
the mother tongue

rostros y manos
lo mejor del cuadro

¿de tal palo tal astilla?

                    precoz
enfila pedazos de madera: convoy
                    de camiones
remontando colinas de aserrín
florestas de viruta
bajo el banco de tablones

Su carácter cerril emana
del oculto remolino de su testa:
                              ¿leo?
¿capricornio? ¿piscis?

                Proviene
        de la escuela florentina, no es
        manierista / no
                collage:

¿el maestro de Pujiura?

Tenía un tallercito de media agua
en su propio solar de la calle principal
— arboledas de limón y frutilla —
esos pájaros parecen salidos
de las miniaturas persas

                luz de bodega: siglo XVII
                ¿La Sagrada Familia?

El Padre — un forastero de los valles —
hacía ataúdes de segunda
                        la Madre
Mater Purísima les daba
una mano de pintura
                y el Niño

faces and hands
the best part of the painting

a chip off the old block?

                                    very bright
he links up pieces of wood: convoy
                              of trucks
ascending hills of sawdust
thickets of wood shavings
beneath the bench of broad planks

His headstrong nature springs
from the hidden whorl on his crown
                              Leo?
Capricorn? Pisces?

               This comes
        from the Florentine School, it is not
        mannerist/not
               collage:

The Master of Pujiura?

He used to have a little wood shop
in his own house on the main street
— groves of lime and a strawberry patch —
those birds look like they escaped
from Persian miniatures

                              chiaroscuro: XVII century
                              The Holy Family?

The Father — a foreigner from the valleys —
used to make crude coffins
                        the Mother
Mater Purissima gave them
fresh coats of paint

—que ya sabía escribir—
                              copiaba
los nombres de los difuntos
                sus iniciales
en las cruces en los cajones:

¿una escena votiva?

En el seno materno / Edén
de los pájaros parlantes
el Niño-Dios gatea
                          se encima
por la cohorte de perros perdigueros
que lo guarda:

un angelito murillano
observa la escena

                                    and the Son
— who already knew how to write—
                                              used to inscribe
the names of the deceased
            their initials
on the crosses and the coffins:

a votive scene?

Upon the maternal bosom / Eden
of chattering birds
the Christ Child crawls
                    clambers over
a pack of hounds
that protect him:

a little Murillesque angel
observes the scene

NOTES

Calca is a town in Peru's Sacred Valley in the Cusco region.

The Master of Pujiura was an Andean painter active during the late sixteenth century.

SAN JOSÉ, LA VIRGEN Y EL NIÑO
LUCAS YAULLI
Templo de Maca

En el trío de la Sagrada Familia
siempre fui el menos importante:

    el binomio Madre-Niño
                lleva
sendas aureolas en la testa
            y viste
telas de damasco carmesí

Mi modesto taller de carpintero
las herramientas desgastadas
            fue
fueron
lo único que legué a mi hijo:

la sierra de vueltas, las garlopas
         de pino
el gramil, las escuadras
el pequeño cepillo *torito*

Barbado y hercúleo
la alzada del Santo tiene
errores de proporción, y el rostro
       de nariz afilada
una expresión rígida

No soy el celestial esposo de María
ni el consorte de *Los desposorios de la Virgen*
Soy el vecino morador de esta villa:
      mi oficio
es hacer puertas, mesas y ataúdes
      es decir
un individuo de siete oficios
y catorce necesidades

SAINT JOSEPH, THE VIRGIN AND THE CHILD
LUCAS YAULLI
Maca Church

In the trio of the Holy Family
I was always the least important

    the Mother-Child binomial
                      carries
halo beams around the head
               and wears
drapes of scarlet damask

My modest carpenter's workshop
the worn-down tools
              was
were
all that I bequeathed to my son:

a hand saw, the planers
             of pine
the marking gauge, the framing squares
the tiny wood shaver called "little bull"

Bearded and herculean
the Saint's body has
errors of proportion, and the face
       with its sharp nose
a rigid expression

I am not Mary's celestial spouse
nor the consort in *The Betrothal of the Virgin*
I am the village handyman:
       my job
is to make doors, tables and coffins
       I mean
a fellow with seven trades
and fourteen needs

Siempre quise tener un par de bueyes
                    aradores
un bosquecillo de eucaliptos donde
ningún pájaro anida: la fuerte
                    fragancia del árbol
es letal para los pichones

Sobre un lecho de aserrín
el buen Niño duerme
y sus padres velan

Con resignación o recelo
la estirpe de María me llama *El viejo*
y a ella *La terneja*

La Virgen inclina el cuello
con la misma gracia pagana que Venus
saliendo del mar

No obstante mi discreto rol
¿paternidad responsable?
                    permanezco
en algunos cuadros de devoción:

          Los primeros pasos del Niño Jesús
          San José y la Virgen buscan posada
                La huida a Egipto,
                              etc.

I always wanted to have a pair of oxen
                for plowing
a little grove of eucalyptus where
no bird made its nest: the strong
                fragrance of the tree
being lethal to hatchlings

Upon a bed of sawdust
the Good Child sleeps
and his parents watch over him

With resignation or distrust
Mary's family calls me *The Old Man*
and her *The Calf*

The Virgin inclines her neck
with the same pagan grace as Venus
emerging from the sea

In spite of my discreet role
responsible for paternity?
                I remain
in some devotional scenes:

        The first steps of the Baby Jesus
        Saint Joseph and the Virgin in search of an inn
            The flight to Egypt,
                        etc.

NOTES

Lucas Yaulli was a School of Cusco painter active during the seventeenth century.

Maca is a village in Peru's Colca Canyon, near the city of Arequipa.

JUICIO, GLORIA Y PENAS
DE LOS CONDENADOS
TADEO ESCALANTE
Murales de Huaro y Andahuaylillas

Cintas parlantes salen de la boca
de un moribundo

> *velad*
> *porque no sabéis a qué hora*
> *vendrá el Señor*

Arco triunfal:
frutales de Yucay, de Amberes
—microclima perfecto—
⠀⠀⠀⠀⠀⠀⠀⠀⠀⠀¿el averno?

Entonces vi una mujer montada
sobre una bestia roja
de siete cabezas y dos cuernos

> En los muros del ábside
> en el friso del coro
> ⠀⠀⠀⠀*La Sixtina de América*
> Las postrimerías del hombre: muerte
> juicio, infierno y gloria

⠀⠀⠀⠀⠀⠀⠀⠀⠀⠀⠀⠀⠀⠀⠀⠀⠀⠀*Ven*

te mostraré
el juicio de la gran ramera
sentada sobre dos aguas

⠀⠀⠀⠀⠀⠀⠀Luz negra:
⠀⠀⠀⠀⠀⠀⠀sapos y serpientes devoran
⠀⠀⠀⠀⠀⠀⠀el sexo de los lujuriosos

En el tormento de la rueda ardiente
giran los soberbios y orgullosos

JUDGMENT, SALVATION AND
THE SUFFERING OF THE DAMNED
TADEO ESCALANTE
Murals in Huaro and Andahuaylillas

Ribbons of speech exit the mouth
of a dying man

    take heed
    because ye know not at what hour
    the Lord will come

Triumphal arch
orchards of Yucay, of Antwerp
  —an ideal microclimate—
                  the underworld?

Then I saw a woman mounted
upon a red beast
with seven heads and two horns

    On the walls of the apse
    on the frieze of the choir
        The Sistine Chapel of America
    The four last things of man: death
    judgment, hell, and heaven

                  Come
I will show you
the judging of the Great Whore
seated on two waters

          In shadow light:
          toads and serpents devour
          the sex of the lustful

In the torture of the burning wheel
rotate the arrogant and the proud

Ay de mí que ardiendo quedo
Ay que pude y ya no puedo
Ay que por siempre he de arder
Ay que a Dios nunca he de ver

¿padre Bocanegra?

Escena marginal:

mientras el pintor alista la tela
un ángel arcabucero aguarda
limpiando su arma en el taller:
Cuesta de San Blas
Cusco

Desciende un carruaje de fuego
en los trigales de Huaro

Nave izquierda:

Después de la muerte hay dos caminos:
infierno y gloria / el primero
cubierto de rosas / el otro
sembrado de espinas

¿naif?

¿naturalismo italiano?

Desde la región celeste
un arcángel arpista
rasguea tonadas

Ay me that I stay here burning
Ay that I could have and no longer can
Ay that forever I must burn
Ay that God I must never see

Father Bocanegra?

Marginal scene:

as the painter prepares the canvas
a harquebusier angel waits
cleaning his weapon in the studio:
San Blas Hill
Cusco

A fiery chariot descends
upon the wheat fields of Huaro

Left nave:

After death there are two roads:
hell and heaven/the first
covered with roses/the other
sown with thorns

naïve art?

Italian naturalism?

In the heaven corner
an archangel with a harp
strums tunes

NOTES

Huaro is a town outside of Cusco. Huaro's church contains elaborate religious murals by Tadeo Escalante.

Andahuaylillas is a small Andean village near Cusco. Its church, which many call the Sistine Chapel of America, is known for its many treasures including gold leaf frescos and a gilded altar. Originally built in the seventeenth century, the church

contains works by Diego Quispe Tito, Tadeo Escalante, and others.

Tadeo Escalante was a mestizo Cusqueñan painter and muralist active during the late eighteenth and early nineteenth centuries. He painted many depictions of hell.

Yucay is a town located in Peru's Sacred Valley near Cusco.

Antwerp, Belgium was a center for the copying and exportation of great works of European art. Many of these copies were shipped to South America.

Padre Bocanegra, Juan Pérez Bocanegra, was a Spanish priest stationed in Andahuaylillas during the sixteenth century. He composed religious hymns in Quechua and also wrote the *Manual sacramental del evangelio cristiano, The Holy Guidebook of Christianity.*

Two waters refers to a concept in Andean religion. It is said that there are two types of water. One is clean and crystalline, which is blessed or holy water and associated with God. The other is dark and murky water, which is associated with the devil.

San Blas Hill is a narrow steep street in Cusco. Today many artists and craftspeople have their studios there.

EL OBSERVADOR DE LOS CIELOS
Detalle
CÍRCULO DE FRANCISCO WILLKA
Conjunto Mural de Checacupe / Juicio Final

Así
se tiene mandado que no sólo en las iglesias
ni en lugares públicos ni secretos de los pueblos de indios
se pinte el sol, la luna ni las estrellas
por quitarles la ocasión de volver —como está dicho—
a sus antiguos delirios y disparates

1.
parcelas de trigo
plantíos de papa
rojos quinuales
          en flor

acecha de noche
la errante constelación
el *ojo de la llama*

2.
luz de bengala
refulge el *zorro*
en el sagrado *corral*
de las llamas albinas

a sus anchas arrea
airado mastín
a la mansa tropilla

3.
bombarda roja
relumbra fugaz
en la puerta añil
del arco iris:

THE WATCHER OF THE SKIES
Detail
CIRCLE OF FRANCISCO WILLKA
Mural Series, Checacupe / The Last Judgment

Henceforth
it is strictly commanded that neither in the churches
nor in public places nor in the hidden areas of Indian villages
may one paint the sun, the moon or the stars
for this prevents them from returning—as it is said—
to their ancient whirlings and wanderings

1.

plots of wheat
patches of potatoes
red quinoa clusters
                    in bloom

at night approaches
the roving constellation
the *eye of the llama*

2.

a dazzling flare
the *fox* shines brightly
in the sacred *corral*
of the albino llamas

nipping at their flanks
the fierce mastiff
drives the gentle flock

3.

red fireworks
fleeting blaze
under the indigo arch
of the rainbow:

la llama arrodillada
¿y su cría que lacta?

4.
la mancha fatal
de los dos sapos
los apareados
(bulto de niebla)
empaña la luna
(barca de niebla)

no Osa Mayor
no Cruz del Sur

5.
en las nubes dispersas
a ratos anida
la sola *perdiz*

the kneeling llama
and her calf that suckles?

4.

the fatal stain
of the two toads
the breeding pair
(veil of fog)
obscures the moon
(boat of fog)

not the Great Bear
not the Southern Cross

5.

in the scattered clouds
nests now and then
the lone *partridge*

NOTES

Checacupe is in the Cusco region. Its church dates from the seventeenth century. It was near Checacupe that Tupac Amaru, the Inca rebel leader, was defeated by the Spanish in 1572.

Francisco Willka, also known as Lucas Ullka (Willka), was a Cusco school painter born in Checacupe in 1651.

EL EJÉRCITO DE DIOS
ANÓNIMO
Convento de Ocopa

Arco toral
        trascoro
cenefa interior de la capilla:

"El traidor
elevó la mirada hacia Él
como quien indaga un árbol
por un fruto maduro"

      Iluminación dramática:

Sobre un fondo bucólico
—terrazas de Pisac, de Korikancha—
                      Zaafiel
el ángel de los vientos y los huracanes
discurre
        ¿charla?
con el que sostiene el rayo
de la furia divina:

sus maneras denotan
pasos de ballet
           el vuelo de paños
regias carnaciones

una ráfaga de aire pasa
entre los personajes

El encuentro de dos hombres es el encuentro
de dos ríos, dice
en la divisa de un serafín

pájaros parlantes, aves canoras colman
los aires del séptimo cielo:

THE ARMY OF GOD
ANONYMOUS
Ocopa Convent

Transverse arch
      choir screen
the chapel's interior border:

"The traitor
lifted his gaze toward Him
as one who searches a tree
for ripe fruit"

      Dramatic lighting:

Upon a pastoral background
—terraces of Pisac, of Korikancha—
                       Zaphiel
the angel of winds and hurricanes
passes by
    shoots the breeze?
with another who bears the lightning bolt
of divine fury:

his movements call to mind
ballet steps
           the fluttering of veils
regal flesh and blood

a gust of wind blows
between the figures

The meeting of two men is the meeting
of two rivers, proclaims
the shield of a seraph

chattering birds, warblers fill
the skies of the seventh heaven:

¿tendales de Warán
de Challapampa?

El ángel que porta una brizna
                    de olivo
—rica túnica, peto de cuero—

alza vuelo al primer plano:
                        Ángel-virtud
venciendo la avaricia

las anchas bocamangas / los borceguíes
                            que calza
son de origen sarraceno

llena la simetría
una roca ficticia
                    ¿la piedra cansada?

Al fondo:
            ráfagas de brillantes carmines
                        y bermellones
                                    no
paisajismo tenebrista
no camión portatropas:

ángeles / soldados resplandecientes
guardan la armonía de los cielos:

Rafael: Sanador de Dios
Gabriel: Fuerza de María
Miguel: ¿Quién como Dios?

the granaries of Warán?
the barns of Challapampa?

The angel that carries a twig
        from an olive tree
—ornate tunic, leather breastplate—

springs forth to the frontlines:
                                Mighty-Angel
defeating the greedy

the broad gauntlets / the buskins
                        he wears
are of Saracen origin

to complete the symmetry
an imaginary boulder
                the tired stone?

In the background:
                bursts of gleaming carmine
                        and vermillion
                                        no
tenebrist landscape
no wagon full of soldiers

angels/resplendent soldiers
guard the harmony of the heavens:

Raphael: Healer of God
Gabriel: Mary's Strength
Michael: He who is like God?

NOTES

The *Ocopa Convent* was built by Spanish Franciscan priests in 1725 as a base from which to convert the indigenous people to Catholicism. The convent is located in the town of Santa Rosa de Ocopa in the highland region of Junín, about 680 miles (1109 kilometers) northwest of Cusco.

Pisac is a village in the Sacred Valley near Cusco.

Korikancha is the Inca Temple of the Sun located in the center of Cusco.

Zaphiel is an angel found in the non-canonical book of Enoch.

Warán is a little village in Peru's Sacred Valley.

Challapampa is, in this case, a village in the Sacred Valley. Numerous villages in Peru are named Challapampa.

The tired stone is a reference to a Quechua legend concerning the construction of Sacsayhuamán, a site outside of Cusco. In this legend, workers during Inca times were hoisting a large boulder to fit into the stonework. The boulder could not be hauled by the workers to Cusco due to its great weight, and to this day the stone stands in its original place, a long way from Cusco.

About the Poet

PHOTO: Juha Varvikko

ODI GONZALES, born in Cusco, Peru, is an award-winning poet who writes in both Quechua and Spanish. He holds a degree in Literature from the Universidad Nacional de San Agustín de Arequipa, an MA in Latin American literature from the University of Maryland and a PhD from the Universidad Nacional Mayor de San Marcos.

In collaboration with English-speaking writers and academics, Gonzales has translated into English a significant body of work on the Peruvian oral tradition, including myths, legends, and rituals, for the Smithsonian Museum of the American Indian in Washington, D. C., National Geographic Television, and The National Foreign Language Center at the University of Maryland. Gonzales is a frequent presenter at indigenous language conferences and Latin American poetry festivals. His poems and translations from the Quechua appear in several prominent anthologies, among them *The FSG Book of Twentieth-Century Latin American Poetry* and *The Oxford Book of Latin American Poetry*.

From 1990 to 2000, Gonzales taught at Universidad Nacional de San Agustín de Arequipa. Since 2000, he has divided his time between Peru and the US. He currently teaches courses in Quechua language and culture and prehispanic literature of the Andean region at New York University. Gonzales is the author of seven poetry collections. *Birds on the Kiswar Tree* is his first collection to be published in a bilingual Spanish and English edition.⌘

About the Translator

PHOTO: Beverly Collins-Roberts

LYNN LEVIN is a poet, writer, and translator. She is the author of four collections of poems: *Miss Plastique* (Ragged Sky Press, 2013), *Fair Creatures of an Hour* (Loonfeather Press, 2009), *Imaginarium* (Loonfeather Press, 2005), and *A Few Questions about Paradise* (Loonfeather Press, 2000). She is co-author of a craft-of-poetry text, *Poems for the Writing: Prompts for Poets* (Texture Press, 2013).

Her poems have appeared in *Ploughshares, Boulevard, Washington Square Review, Hopkins Review, Artful Dodge, Connecticut Review, Verse Daily,* on Garrison Keillor's *The Writer's Almanac,* and in anthologies such as *Rabbit Ears: TV Poems* (Poets Wear Prada, 2014) and *The Bloomsbury Anthology of Contemporary Jewish American Poetry* (Bloomsbury Publishing, 2013).

Born in St. Louis, Missouri, Levin holds a BA in comparative literature from Northwestern University and an MFA from Vermont College of Fine Arts. A former producer of the TV talk show, *The Drexel InterView,* she is a lecturer in creative writing at the University of Pennsylvania and an adjunct associate professor of English at Drexel University.⌘

Other Books by 2Leaf Press

2LEAF PRESS challenges the status quo by publishing alternative fiction, non-fiction, poetry and bilingual works by activists, academics, poets and authors dedicated to diversity and social justice with scholarship that is accessible to the general public. 2LEAF PRESS produces high quality and beautifully produced hardcover, paperback and ebook formats through our series: *2LP Explorations in Diversity, 2LP University Books, 2LP Classics, 2LP Translations, Nuyorican World Series,* and *2LP Current Affairs, Culture & Politics.* Below is a selection of 2LEAF PRESS' published titles.

2LP EXPLORATIONS IN DIVERSITY

Substance of Fire: Gender and Race in the College Classroom
by Claire Millikin
Foreword by R. Joseph Rodríguez, Afterword by Richard Delgado
Contributed material by Riley Blanks, Blake Calhoun, Rox Trujillo

Black Lives Have Always Mattered
A Collection of Essays, Poems, and Personal Narratives
Edited by Abiodun Oyewole

The Beiging of America:
Personal Narratives about Being Mixed Race in the 21st Century
Edited by Cathy J. Schlund-Vials, Sean Frederick Forbes, Tara Betts
with an Afterword by Heidi Durrow

What Does it Mean to be White in America?
Breaking the White Code of Silence, A Collection of Personal Narratives
Edited by Gabrielle David and Sean Frederick Forbes
Introduction by Debby Irving and Afterword by Tara Betts

2LP UNIVERSITY BOOKS
Designs of Blackness, Mappings in the Literature and
Culture of African Americans
A. Robert Lee
20TH ANNIVERSARY EXPANDED EDITION

2LP CLASSICS
Adventures in Black and White
Edited and with a critical introduction by Tara Betts
by Philippa Duke Schuyler

Monsters: Mary Shelley's Frankenstein and Mathilda
by Mary Shelley, edited by Claire Millikin Raymond

2LP TRANSLATIONS
Birds on the Kiswar Tree
by Odi Gonzales, Translated by Lynn Levin
Bilingual: English/Spanish

Incessant Beauty, A Bilingual Anthology
by Ana Rossetti, Edited and Translated by Carmela Ferradáns
Bilingual: English/Spanish

NUYORICAN WORLD SERIES
Our Nuyorican Thing, The Birth of a Self-Made Identity
by Samuel Carrion Diaz, with an Introduction by Urayoán Noel
Bilingual: English/Spanish

Hey Yo! Yo Soy!, 40 Years of Nuyorican Street Poetry,
The Collected Works of Jesús Papoleto Meléndez
Bilingual: English/Spanish

LITERARY NONFICTION
No Vacancy; Homeless Women in Paradise
by Michael Reid

The Beauty of Being, A Collection of Fables, Short Stories & Essays
by Abiodun Oyewole

WHEREABOUTS: Stepping Out of Place,
An Outside in Literary & Travel Magazine Anthology
Edited by Brandi Dawn Henderson

PLAYS
Rivers of Women, The Play
by Shirley Bradley LeFlore, with photographs by Michael J. Bracey

AUTOBIOGRAPHIES/MEMOIRS/BIOGRAPHIES
Trailblazers, Black Women Who Helped Make America Great
American Firsts/American Icons
by Gabrielle David

Mother of Orphans
The True and Curious Story of Irish Alice, A Colored Man's Widow
by Dedria Humphries Barker

Strength of Soul
by Naomi Raquel Enright

Dream of the Water Children:
Memory and Mourning in the Black Pacific
by Fredrick D. Kakinami Cloyd
Foreword by Velina Hasu Houston, Introduction by Gerald Horne
Edited by Karen Chau

The Fourth Moment: Journeys from the Known to the Unknown, A Memoir
by Carole J. Garrison, Introduction by Sarah Willis

POETRY
PAPOLÍTICO, Poems of a Political Persuasion
by Jesús Papoleto Meléndez
with an Introduction by Joel Kovel and DeeDee Halleck

Critics of Mystery Marvel, Collected Poems
by Youssef Alaoui, with an Introduction by Laila Halaby

shrimp
by jason vasser-elong, with an Introduction by Michael Castro
The Revlon Slough, New and Selected Poems
by Ray DiZazzo, with an Introduction by Claire Millikin

Written Eye: Visuals/Verse
by A. Robert Lee

A Country Without Borders: Poems and Stories of Kashmir
by Lalita Pandit Hogan, with an Introduction by Frederick Luis Aldama

Branches of the Tree of Life
The Collected Poems of Abiodun Oyewole 1969-2013
by Abiodun Oyewole, edited by Gabrielle David
with an Introduction by Betty J. Dopson

2Leaf Press is an imprint owned and operated by the Intercultural Alliance of Artists & Scholars, Inc. (IAAS), a NY-based nonprofit organization that publishes and promotes multicultural literature.

NEW YORK
www.2leafpress.org